THE COMPLETE BOOK OF
DRESSING UP

THE COMPLETE BOOK OF
DRESSING UP

Step-by-step projects for fabulous fun costumes

by

JULIET MOXLEY

EBURY PRESS
LONDON

For Alice and Jessica

This edition first published in 1996

1 3 5 7 9 10 8 6 4 2

Text © 1996 Juliet Moxley
Photography © 1993, 1996 Ebury Press

Juliet Moxley has asserted her right to be identified as the author of this book.

All rights reserved. No part of this publication may be reproduced, stored
in a retrieval system, or transmitted in any form or by any means, electronic, mechanical,
photocopying, recording or otherwise, without the prior permission of the copyright owners.

This edition first published in 1996 by Ebury Press,
Random House, 20 Vauxhall Bridge Road, London SW1V 2SA

Random House Australia (Pty) Limited
20 Alfred Street, Milsons Point, Sydney,
New South Wales 2061, Australia

Random House New Zealand Limited
18 Poland Street, Glenfield,
Auckland 10, New Zealand

Random House South Africa (Pty) Limited
PO Box 337, Bergvlei, South Africa

Random House UK Limited Reg. No. 954009

Some of the material in this book was previously published in *Children's Parties* by Juliet Moxley.

A CIP catalogue record for this book is available from the British Library.

Editors: Emma Callery and Krystyna Green
Design: Jerry Goldie Graphic Design
Photographs: Marie-Louise Avery and Lucy Tizard
Illustrator: Kate Simunek

ISBN 0 09 181403 0

Printed and bound in Portugal by Printer Portugesa, Lisbon

Papers used by Ebury Press are natural recyclable products made from wood grown in
sustainable forests.

The Publishers and Author would like to thank the following:
Pelikan UK Ltd for supplying fabric paints and pens
Dylon for supplying fabric pens, putty and glitter paint
Ells and Farrier for supplying beads and sequins
Paper Chase for supplying streamers and paper
Labeena Ishaque for hand modelling and general assistance
Jill Sheridan for the party games
Elna for the loan of their sewing machine
Cecilie Halvorson, Monica Syversen, Rachel Collins, Karin Werstrom, Diana
Hallstrom, Sian Murphy, Sasha Haworth, Oliver, Jessica and Alice Moxley, Anna and
Christina Ashford, Carlene Mills, Zander, Oliver Fare, Ping and Gee Lou, Katherine,
Edward and Anthony Saunt, Sophie Hallstrom, Maria Dunn and Amy Bridge for being
such wonderful and co-operative models.

CONTENTS

INTRODUCTION

Children of all ages love dressing up. They might have been invited to a fancy dress party or simply want to play with friends or on their own in a make-believe world. Whatever the occasion, 'pretending' or acting out an adventure is much more fun if you are wearing the right disguise. Younger children in particular love it when you say 'I can't see so-and-so anywhere, but who's this handsome cowboy?' or whatever.

Of course, it is possible to buy ready-made costumes but these are often expensive and the price prohibitive, especially if you have more than one child. This book is full of costumes that are easy and inexpensive to make. My qualifications for writing it are that I am a working mother with four children who have all wanted to dress up as something or other over the last fifteen years. I have had lots of practice at creating outfits!

Many of the costumes can be made using old sheets, curtains, worn-out clothes, or off-cuts of material. Some take a little time to make but you don't need to be an expert with a sewing machine for all the costumes. For instance, if you don't want to make a complete animal body out of fake fur (using the all-in-one pattern that can be adapted to make almost any costume), your child will feel just as dressed up by wearing leggings or tights and a top in the relevant colour, together with a tail and perhaps a hood with animal ears.

I have also included some dressing-up props that complete the picture and that children can help with. Fairies need magic wands with glittery stars on top; butterflies can have wings decorated with shapes cut out of coloured paper; and it is simple to make a glittering crown or cheerful clown's hat once you know how. Fancy dress parties are often the reason that children dress up, so I have suggested a few games and things for children to do while they are in their costumes – it all adds to the fun.

Getting Started

Before you begin to make a costume, think about what is involved, what is going to be the simplest for you and what is going to fit in with your lifestyle. If you are very busy, don't try to make everything yourself but rope in other help from willing hands, however young they are. Even little ones can hold a paintbrush and sprinkle glitter on to glue.

Another thing to consider is what materials you have to hand. If you have lots of red fabric, then perhaps your daughter would like to dress up as Little Red Riding Hood – the cloak is very straightforward. Similarly, it doesn't take long to transform green material into a dinosaur or elf costume. Or, rather than go out and make a special purchase, you might be able to dye an old sheet or shirt to the shade you want. And remember that you can often pick up useful garments and assorted fabric oddments at jumble sales and charity shops (so long as you have got somewhere you can store them without taking up valuable space at home). It's also a good idea to keep a selection of old buttons, metallic wrappers and so on – there's no end to the ways you can use these to add interest to an outfit.

Whichever costumes you decide to make, I hope your children enjoy dressing up in them as much as mine have done.

Juliet Moxley

SPRINGTIME CREATURES

After a long grey winter, why not celebrate the arrival of spring with these brightly coloured animal outfits? Just think what fun it will be dressing up as an Easter chick or bunny on Easter Day. You could have your very own Easter Parade at home where everyone has to make their own special bonnet decorated with paper flowers and ribbons, and later you can have a competition to choose the best one. The winner, of course, gets a chocolate egg!

Making the Costumes

Making a Bunny Tail

1 Place a saucer on the back of white fake fur and, using a crayon, draw around it. Cut out the circle.

2 Using a needle and thread, sew running stitches around the edge of the circle.

3 Draw up the running stitches so that the fur is gathered into a fluffy round tail shape. Secure by knotting the two ends of the thread together and, using a safety pin, attach the tail to the bunny.

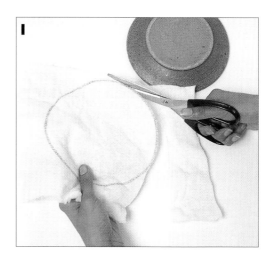

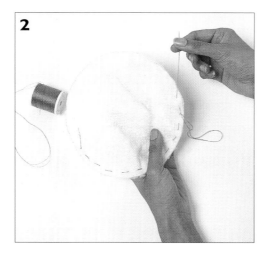

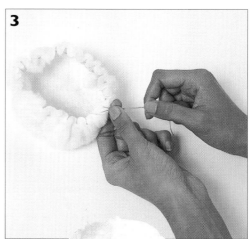

★ For a bunny head, use the hood pattern on page 61 and make it in white fur with long ears attached. The ears are very simple to make: cut two long ear shapes from white fur and two pink felt linings. Stitch the pink felt to the ears and then stitch the ears on either side of the hood.

★ Finish off the bunny outfit by wearing a white T-shirt or sweat shirt and tights.

★ Make a chicken hood from yellow fake fur with a yellow/orange beak attached. Make the beak out of two pieces of triangular felt and a piece of interfacing. Wear a yellow T-shirt and tights to complete the outfit.

Other Ideas

★ Make a lamb hood from woolly fake fur, and its tail from a long piece of fake fur. Complete the outfit by wearing a white T-shirt and tights.
★ Make an Easter crown from fake flowers wired together.
★ Make an Easter bonnet by taking an old straw hat and decorating it with different coloured ribbons and paper flowers.

THINGS TO DO

These activities are even more fun if you are dressed up for Easter and have invited friends to a springtime party.

Hunting for eggs

You will need Basket or other container for each child playing the game; selection of small chocolate or sugar-coated eggs – preferably wrapped in shiny paper.

To play Well before the game is to be played, hide all the eggs in the house or garden. Then set the children various tasks such as 'Find three speckled eggs' or 'Find four eggs wrapped in blue paper and three wrapped in silver'. This prevents one child from collecting all the hidden eggs and also means that everyone has something to take home with them.

Animal charades

This is a team game for younger children which requires three or more players per team. It is important to stress before the game starts that no sound effects are allowed.

You will need A list of animals for each team. It is a good idea to give the teams different animals so that players can't pick up hints by watching another team.

To play One child is elected to go first and is secretly told which animal to be. He or she then acts out the animal to his or her team. The team member who guesses correctly goes quickly to the organiser and whispers the name of the animal, and – if correct – is given another animal for the team to guess. Whichever team finishes the whole list first is the winner.

Painting eggs

This is a good activity to keep children occupied while they are waiting for guests to arrive at an Easter party.

You will need Well in advance, hard boil enough eggs (so that all the children will have at least one to decorate plus a few extra); wax crayons (for younger children); wool or string (for older children) plus saucepans filled with different coloured 'dye'. Use red water (from boiled beetroot), yellow water (from onions) and blue water (from red cabbage).

How to proceed Each child selects an egg to decorate. Younger children using wax crayons should be encouraged to colour their eggs with thick patterns as this is easier to do. Older children can wind string or wool around the eggs, fastening the ends securely. Then the eggs need to be left for at least one hour in whichever colour water the child wants. Once the eggs are dry, cut off the string or wool to reveal the pattern.

CIRCUS CLOWNS

To be the star of the show, what could be better than dressing up in a colourful clown outfit? It's easy to adapt existing clothes, perhaps decorating a swimsuit with sequins or using eye-catching braces to hold up a pair of baggy trousers. There are lots of fun and simple-to-make details you can add too – for example, gather a piece of brightly coloured net to tie around the neckline of the clown costume or decorate a hat with pompons.

MAKING THE COSTUMES

★ Make a clown's costume (see previous page) from an all-in-one pattern (see pages 58–60) made from lots of bright fabrics. Cover it in ribbons, add patch pockets and a ribbon ruff collar.

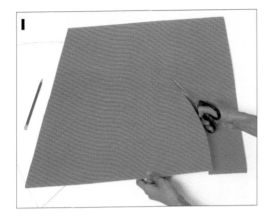

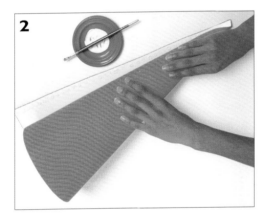

Making a Clown's Hat

1 Using the template on page 62 as a guide, draw the shape of the hat on to a piece of coloured card and cut out.

2 Roll the card into a cone shape and secure the edges with glue or double-sided sticky tape.

3 Glue pompons around the edge and front of the hat. You can fasten a piece of elastic to the sides of the hat so the child can secure it under the chin.

Clown Shoes

False shoes for a clown can be easily and quickly made from card. Place a shoe on a large piece of card and draw an enlarged shoe shape in front and behind it. Cut out the large shoe shape and also cut a hole in the centre of the card for the foot to fit through. Paint the card whatever colour you like – brown, white, black, a mixture – and then draw laces and a shoe tongue and paint on a patch. Make a second shoe and wear them over ordinary shoes. Just make sure it isn't raining if they are going to be worn outside!

Other Ideas

★ Paint a clown face using face paints: make a big mouth and rosy cheeks.

★ Why not continue with the 'all the fun of the circus' theme? A ring master costume is easily adapted from an old tail jacket and top hat. A bow tie will complete the outfit.

★ Be a weight lifter in a swimsuit with a broomstick with balloons tied on either end.

★ To be an acrobat, wear a leotard decorated with sequins and diamanté.

★ If you are inviting friends round for a circus party, it is easy to decorate paper plates with clown faces to make tea time more special. Simply cut out coloured sticky paper for the eyes and mouth and don't forget to add a bright red nose for each. You could also turn the plate into a clown mask, by cutting holes for the eyes to see through and attaching a piece of elastic to hold the plate around the head over the ears.

GAMES TO PLAY

Pass the hats

This game is quite difficult for very young children to play, so I have also included a simplified version that they will be able to manage.

You will need Enough hats so that each child has got one to wear; tape machine with music cassettes.

To play The children wear their hats and stand in a circle facing the back of the child standing to their right. While the music is playing, each child takes the hat off the person in front of them and puts it on their own head. Everyone carries on doing this until the music stops. Do this several times so everyone knows what to do, then remove one hat and let the game begin. This time, when the music stops the person left without a hat on their head is out. Each time a person is out, remove another hat from the circle. When there are only two children left, they should face each other. The winner is the child left wearing the hat.

An alternative for very young children is to throw the hats into the middle of the circle, making sure there is one hat short. When the music stops, the children quickly pick up a hat and put it on. The child without a hat is out. Another hat should be removed from the pile and so the game continues.

Pass the parcel - with a difference

This is unlike the traditional game of pass the parcel and much less messy because it does not involve lots of layers of paper.

You will need Two parcels wrapped in the ordinary way – one should be a prize and the other a booby prize; tape machine with music cassettes.

To play The children sit in a circle on the floor and the two parcels should be handed to children opposite each other. The parcels should be passed on in the same direction as each other until the music stops, when the children holding the parcels are out. This continues until only two players are left. These two pass the parcels between them and open the one in their hands when the music stops.

GHOSTS, GHOULS

AND **W**ITCHES

Whether trick or treating or running around and going bump in the night, Halloween is the perfect occasion for dressing up and frightening your friends. Halloween costumes are varied and easy to make – try creating a mummy made from loo paper, a ghost from a sheet and a witch's hat from a black card cone. Props can be constructed from simple cutouts of bats, pumpkins and black cats. Don't forget a witch also needs a broom to pretend to ride on.

Making the Costumes

★ **For a witch, make a hat as described (right) and make a cloak by following the instructions below.**

Making a Witch's Cloak

1 To make a full cloak you will need a large square of black fabric. Fold the square in half and then in half again. Draw a small curve in the folded corner for the neck and a large curve on the outer edge for the hem. Cut along the curves.

2 Open out the material. You will have a large circle with a hole in the centre. Cut a straight line from the small circle to the edge of the fabric. This will be the front of the cloak. For the collar, cut a length of fabric to fit the neckline and sew on to the cloak. Attach a red ribbon tie to the collar of the cloak and neaten the hem with running stitch.

3 Cut out tissue lamé stars and moons and appliqué them all over the cloak.

1

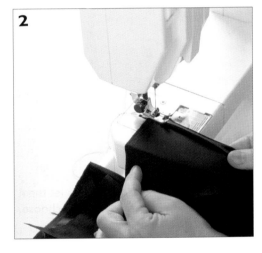

2

3

Making Witches' hats

Witches' hats are fun to make. Draw around a large dinner plate on to a piece of black card. Cut out the circle and then cut it in half – each half makes one hat. Take one half and roll into a cone, gluing the two edges together. To make the brim, measure the circumference of the cone and cut out another circle with the circumference 5cm (2in) wider. Draw a circle 7.5cm (3in) in from the edge and cut along this line. Discard the inner circle. You are now left with a cardboard hoop. At even intervals along this hoop, cut incisions to a depth of 2.5cm (1in). Bend back at right angles and stick to the inside of the hat. Finish off each hat by sticking on gold and silver stars.

Making a Halloween Mask

You can help the children make their personalized Halloween face. All you need are brown paper bags or paper plates, empty yogurt pots containing glue, lolly sticks or brushes with which to use the glue, milk bottle tops, lengths of wool in various colours, thick wax crayons, scissors, string, coloured straws, gold and silver stars and gold and silver felt-tipped pens.

Help the child make holes for eyes and mouth in the paper bag or plate and then let them decorate the mask in any way they choose, using the materials provided. Hair can be added by using lengths of wool which can be glued to the bag or plate above the eyes or down the sides. Paper bags can be worn over the head while plates can be held up in front of the face or secured around the back of the head with a piece of elastic.

Other Ideas

★ Make a ghost from an old sheet with two eye holes cut out and rimmed with black paint.

★ A skeleton can be made using a black T-shirt and tights with bones made from crêpe paper or vylene sewn or stuck on.

★ A severed hand can be made from an old rubber glove with bits of rice crispies (warts) and hair stuck on. Paint the whole thing green – it is truly revolting!

★ You can make a pair of devil's horns by moulding two pieces of red plasticine on to pipe cleaners and then twisting the pipe cleaners on to a head-band.

★ Be a cobweb by wearing shirring elastic over a leotard and tights and add a plastic spider for good measure to be extra frightening.

Into Outer Space

From the man in the moon to astronauts and aliens, the idea of rockets, stars and galaxies always grabs the imagination of children. Bicycle or crash helmets make convincing space helmets, wellies can be sprayed silver and sticking tin foil over cardboard is an easy way to make a spacesuit. Props can be made by using recycled tin foil dishes and milk bottle tops.

MAKING THE COSTUMES

★ For a spaceman (see photograph on previous page), wear a tabard (see page 57) in grey or metallic fabric over white or silver tights and a T-shirt.

★ An alien (see photograph on previous page) can be made by covering a balloon with papier-mâché, gluing on bits of egg box and cutting out a space for the head. Spray the whole thing in silver.

Robot man

A robot made from cardboard boxes is a really effective space companion. Use a large box for the body and then stick on a smaller one for the head and even smaller ones for the arms, legs and feet – shoe boxes are ideal for this. Decorate by either spraying with silver or covering with tin foil and sticking on old tin cans, bits of tubing, cogs and so on. To dress up as a robot, wear a decorated box round your middle, leaving holes for your arms, legs and neck.

Spray painting instructions

1 To decorate anything on a galaxy theme, draw a star on newspaper and cut it out with scissors to make a stencil.

2 Cover your work surface with paper to prevent it becoming covered with paint. Hold the stencil down firmly on to whatever you are decorating and spray with silver paint.

3 To give a golden aura to planets, make a stencil in the same way but use gold paint. Always lift up the stencil carefully when you have finished spraying.

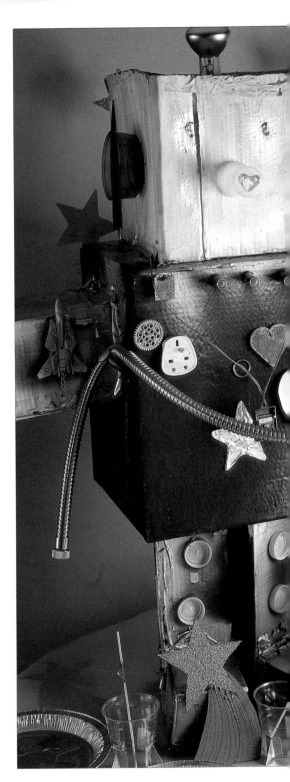

Other Ideas

★ Make a backpack from a cardboard box covered in silver foil attached with elastic shoulder straps.

★ For a robot, wear a tabard (see page 57) in metallic fabric with tinsel, milk bottle tops, bits of tubing and silver foil shapes glued or sewn on. Spray a brown paper bag with silver paint and cut out holes for the eyes and mouth. Wear wellies sprayed with silver paint as space boots.

★ Wear a motorbike helmet.

★ For the man in the moon, cut out a cardboard crescent moon and paint it silver. Attach it with straps to the chest and wear with grey tights and a sweater beneath.

★ A star costume can be made from a star-shaped piece of cardboard sprayed with silver and lengths of tinsel stuck all around the edges.

★ For a star headdress, use a headband with wire attached which has been bent into a star shape and wrapped in tinsel.

GAMES TO PLAY

Here are a few games that children aged seven or eight and above will enjoy while dressed as spacemen and astronauts.

Planet plodding

You will need Two inflated balloons, both attached to 60 cm (2 ft) lengths of string for each child playing the game.

To play Tie a balloon to each child's ankles and let them practise walking around for a short while (taking care not to burst the balloons). Once the game starts, the idea is to pretend to be walking around testing the planet's surface and while doing this to burst the balloons belonging to any other space explorers by treading or jumping on them. Once both balloons are burst, the child is out. The winner is the last person to have one or two balloons left.

Noises from outer space

This is a quiet game to play either among individuals or between teams.

You will need Various objects with which to make sounds like shutting a book, jangling keys, lighting a match, cutting paper with scissors; pencils and paper for the players to write their answers on.

To play The organiser making the noises hides out of sight with the props and says 'Sound number one' while making the noise. Children should be given enough time to write down what they think the answer is before the next sound is made. The winner is the person who identifies the most noises correctly.

Why not combine dressing up as a scarecrow, snail or flower with a feast? Plan to have a picnic outside in the garden although if the sun refuses to come out, you can always move it indoors. You can even have indoor grass – astroturf can be bought at any DIY store.

MAKING THE COSTUMES

★ Turn yourself into a scarecrow with a mop head, straw or raffia for hair, stuck under an old and battered straw hat.

★ Borrow old and tattered jeans, corduroys or dungarees and wear with old misshapen sweaters or shirts with rips or buttons missing.

★ To make the outfit authentic, stick a wooden spoon (stick end outwards) down your sleeves, with a few bits of straw sticking out.

★ Complete the outfit with an old pair of wellies or walking shoes.

★ Make a snail by wearing grey tights and sweater, and attach a grey globe paper lampshade on the back, held on by grey straps. A long padded tail ending in a point needs to be tied to the waist. For the antennae, attach some pipe cleaners with pompons wired to the ends to a hairband.

Other Ideas

★ A bee costume can be made by dressing in bright yellow tights and a yellow T-shirt painted with black stripes using a fabric pen. Make some antennae with yellow and black pipe cleaners and pompons.

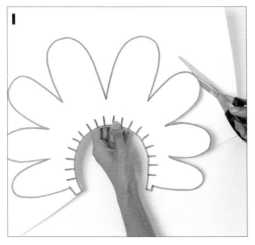

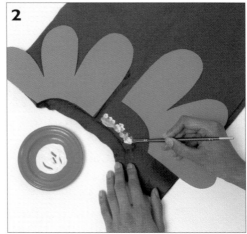

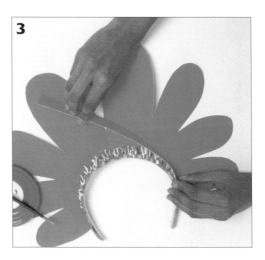

Making a Flower Costume

1 Make a green felt tabard (see instructions on page 57). To make the petal collar for the tabard, cut an A1 sheet of card in half. Using only one half, follow the template on page 63 and draw the petals on the card as shown. Cut out and glue to the front neckline of the tabard.

2 Use the second half of the A1 card to make a petal headpiece. Use the headband template on page 63 as a guide. When you come to cut out the semicircle on the headpiece, cut in little incisions as shown. These will act as tabs which will make it easier to glue the petal headpiece on to a child's headband.

3 Fold out the tabs, apply glue to the headpiece and press the tabs firmly down on the headband. Glue down a long strip of card or material over the headband to hide the glue and stuck down tabs.

A GAME TO PLAY
Musical statues or trees

This is enjoyed by children of all ages and can be played both inside and out.

You will need Tape machine with music cassettes.

To play Everyone dances or runs around while the music is playing. If the game is being played inside, when the music stops all the children must stand as still as possible, pretending to be statues. Anyone who moves is judged to be out. If this is being played outside and there are one or two trees not too far away, the children should run to the nearest tree when the music stops. The last child to reach the safety of a tree is out. This continues until there is just one child left – the winner!

Fairies and Elves

Young children love fairyland. It's where dreams are made and wishes fulfilled. You can have lots of fun making costumes from things around the home. If it's Christmas, you could pretend to be one of Santa's elves, or the fairy on top of the Christmas tree. Add a magical sparkle to your fairy dress with tinsel and glitter.

MAKING THE COSTUMES

★ **For a fairy decorate a leotard with a netting skirt and sequins.**
★ **A full-length petticoat with a frilly nylon skirt can be decorated with glitter.**

Fairy Wings

Make fairy wings from silver card edged with Christmas tinsel and attach them with two elastic straps coming over the shoulders. Alternatively, an effective pair of translucent fairy wings can be created by forming wire coathangers into wing shapes and gluing netting over them. You can also make wings from metallic tissue lamé boned with ridgeline.

A Magic Wand

Make a wand from silver-sprayed dowelling and two star-shaped pieces of card-board covered in glitter or painted silver.

Pixie

★ For a pixie or elf outfit use a tabard of green felt (see page 57) with a zigzag hem with bells attached. Wear it with green or black tights and pixie boots and make a pointed green hat with a bell sewn on to the end.

★ False ears can be made from papier-mâché (see page 56), sewn or stuck on to the sides of the elf's cap.

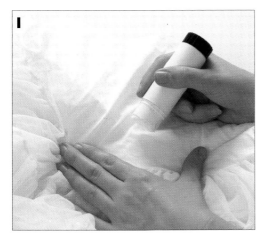

To Decorate a Fairy Dress

1 Attach a net petticoat to a vest or leotard – white or pastel colours are best for a fairy dress. Spread fabric glue evenly along the hem of the petticoat.

2 Cover the work area with paper, then sprinkle silver glitter on to the glued area; shake off the excess glitter. Fill any gaps by resticking and sprinkling on more glitter.

3 Sew, or glue on, silver sequins or diamanté on to the bodice and shoulder straps, and around the neckline of the vest or leotard.

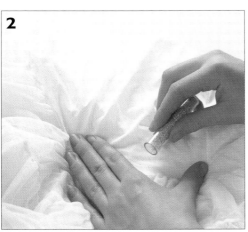

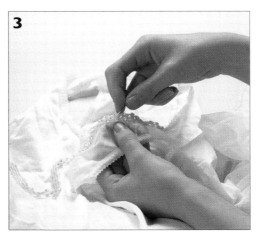

GAMES TO PLAY

What can it be?

You will need Two prizes loosely wrapped in five or six layers of paper with string and sticky tape.

To play The children take it in turns to try to guess what is inside the parcels. Each feels a parcel and is allowed to ask a question which will help them to discover what is inside. Every time a child asks something that proves useful in this quest, one layer of wrapping should be undone. This continues until the last layer is removed and that player is then allowed to keep the prize. More or fewer layers can be wrapped around the parcels depending on the ages of the children (younger ones think the more layers the better) and how long you want the game to last.

Puff ball

You will need One ping pong ball per team; one large straw per player; tape to act as a finishing line.

To play Divide the players into teams which are lined up at one end of the room. Lie the tape on the floor at the other end of the room to mark the finish. Each person at the front of the team puts a ping pong ball on the floor and at the command 'Go' blows the ball along using the straw until they have crossed the finishing line. Then they pick up the ball, run back to the team and give it to the next person who repeats the exercise. The first team to have all players blow the ping pong ball over the line is the winning side.

COWBOYS AND INDIANS

It's great fun to dress up as cowboys and Indians as there are so many different things to be! Indian chiefs, cowgirls or even the Lone Ranger complete with mask and wooden hobby horse. To become a cowboy, decorate old school shirts or jeans with fringing. Bandannas around the neck and a sheriff's star all help to create a Western look.

Making the Costumes

★ A chief's headdress can be made using feathers from a duster sewn on to brown fabric as described to the right.
★ Make a squaw's dress as described below.
★ Use face paints in bright yellows and reds to decorate the squaws' and braves' faces.
★ For a cowboy shirt, use an old school shirt and perhaps add fringing on any pockets.
★ Wear an old denim jacket or a waistcoat.
★ Cowboy hats can be cheaply bought from a toy shop or bend an old fedora trilby into shape.

Cowboy Trousers

Add fringing to a pair of old jeans to make cowboy trousers. Measure the outside leg of the trousers from the waist to the hem. Double this measurement to assess the amount of fringing required. Look for fringing in haberdashery departments; lampshade fringing is ideal. Cut the fringe in half and stick down the outside seam of the jeans using double-sided sticky tape. Alternatively sew the fringing on by hand using running stitch.

A Squaw's Dress

A squaw's dress (right) can be made from a brown tabard (see page 57) of cotton fabric, suedette or real suede. Sew up the sides leaving room for the arms. Cut from the bottom of the skirt up 20cm (8in) at 2.5cm (1in) intervals

to make fringing. Cut a slit of 15cm (6in) in the front of the neck. Cut eye holes and thread them with a brown shoelace. Decorate the neckline with beads or feathers. Add bunches of coloured feathers cut from a feather duster and sew all over the costume. Add coloured buttons to the place where you have sewn on the feathers.

Indian Chief Headdress

1 Cut a piece of brown fabric long enough to tie around the head and come down the sides of the body. Taper the ends. Stick on circles of felt.

2 Remove feathers from brightly coloured feather dusters.

3 Machine the feathers in place using a zigzag stitch.

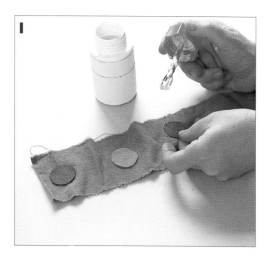

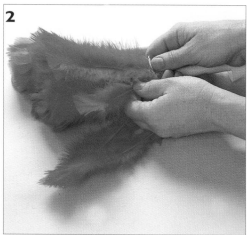

PLAYING COWBOYS AND INDIANS

This is a fun game to play when lots of children are dressed up as cowboys and Indians – though it can get rather noisy!

You will need Lengths of rope or thick string.

To play Divide the children into two teams – one of 'cowboys' and the other 'Indians'. One team member stands separately while the others get into pairs and stand or sit back to back. Each pair should be tied together with several knots. When you shout 'Go', the spare team member has to untie all the knots and free all the captives in his or her team. The first team to have all its members untied is the winner. If the numbers are uneven and one child has not had a go, it is best to play the whole game again. If the game is being played outside, children could be tied to trees or garden furniture instead of each other. Once free, team members can make appropriate noises (whooping and warbling) to encourage the cowboy or Indian doing the untying and add to the excitement.

Other Ideas

★ Jeans can be decorated with fringing down the side.

★ Make a poncho by cutting a hole in the centre of an old blanket or wrap.

★ For a sheriff's badge, cut out a cardboard star and paint it silver. Stick a pin on the back to attach.

Mysterious Mermaid

Make a splash with this shimmering mermaid costume. Use metallic fabrics and netting in the blue-green colours of the sea to create a long fish tail and headdress. Shells collected from the seashore can be used to make a suitable mermaid's necklace or bracelet. Other fun costumes on a seaside theme include a diver, Neptune, or even Mr Punch!

Making the Costume

★ Create a mermaid's costume from a plain pink swimsuit wrapped round with netting to which a padded and appliquéd fish tail is attached (see step-by-step instructions).

★ Stick shells on to blue lamé fabric as a headband.

Making a Mermaid's Tail

1 Draw a tail (see page 62) the length of the wearer from waist to toe and then cut out the shape, twice from metallic fabric and once from a length of wadding. Sew some scales in shiny, metallic fabric on to the tip of the tail.

2 Place the two metallic tail pieces together with shiny sides facing in. Sew down both sides and around the tail. Leave the top open.

3 Turn the material the right way round and insert the wadding. Pin a long length of blue netting to the front of the mermaid's tail. It should be long enough to tie around the waist. Finish off the tail by sewing shut the top.

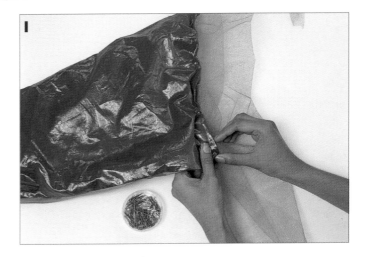

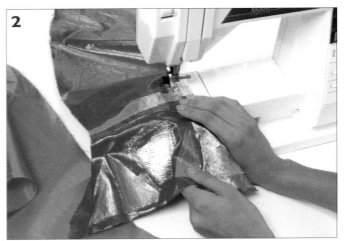

A Mermaid's Necklace

Finish off the mermaid outfit by adding a necklace or bracelet. Paint small pieces of macaroni blue and green and, once dry, thread them on to some cotton and tie around the neck or wrist. Alternatively, glue some seashells on to a length of cotton, spray them gold and tie around the neck.

Other ideas

★ For Neptune, make a tabard (see page 57) from tissue lamé in silver, blue or green, tied with seaweed or a belt made from shells.

★ Make his trident from a piece of card and attach it to silver-sprayed dowelling.

★ Cut fish-shaped masks from card and paint them with tropical fish colours and unusual patterns.

★ To be a diver, wear a snorkel, face mask, and a rubber suit or black leotard.

★ Be a sand castle made from corrugated cardboard with shells and a beached starfish stuck or drawn on. Alternatively you can make a big sandcastle to hide in.

★ Mr Punch's costume can be made by wearing a red cap with a bell, a red ruff, some colourful striped trousers and an enormous papier-mâché nose.

GAMES TO PLAY

Musical islands

This is a great game to play at a party with a seaside theme and is a variation on musical chairs. Two advantages are that you don't need lots of room to accommodate the chairs and also children can help to make the props in advance.
You will need Islands drawn or painted on paper (one for each child playing the game); tape machine with music cassettes.
To play Place the islands on the sea (the floor). When the music plays, the children must move around in the water. As soon as the music stops, they have to run and hop on to an island. When the music starts up again, take away an island while the children are moving around. This time, when the music stops the child who does not land on an island is out. Continue in this way until there are only two children and one island left in the game. This time, when the music stops the first child to step on to the island is the winner. To make the game more complicated, tell the children to stand on one leg when they are on the islands. If they fall into the sea, they are also out of the game.

Squeal mermaid squeal

This is a variation on the old traditional game 'Squeak piggy squeak' which younger children find very amusing.
You will need A cushion and a scarf to be used as a blindfold.
To play Ask for a volunteer to be blindfolded. Once you have checked that the child cannot see, turn him or her around three times. The rest of the children then find a seat in the room (or sit on chairs in a circle around the blindfolded person) and keep very quiet. The blindfolded player is then handed a cushion and moves around until he or she finds someone and puts the cushion on their lap. He or she then sits on the cushion and says 'Squeal mermaid squeal' and must then wait for the player underneath to respond. The blindfolded child has to guess on whose lap he or she is sitting. If the guess is correct, these two then swap places, and if wrong the blindfolded player continues and has another go.

KNIGHTS AND DAMSELS

Why not have a fantasy adventure, with beautiful jewelled costumes and crowns and tiaras? It's a chance to play a fairytale princess or a gallant knight, or be a page boy or damsel in need of rescuing!

Making the Costumes

★ Apart from a long flowing dress, the most important element in a damsel's costume is a pointed conical hat (see right).

★ For the damsel's top, criss-cross a vest bodice with ribbons and add a sequin at each intersection.

★ Make a knight's shield and helmet as described (see right).

★ For a cape, use gold fabric and add a drawstring 5cm (2in) from the top to make a stand-up collar.

★ A glittery crown adds some glamour – see the description below.

Making a Glittery Crown

1 Cut a crown shape out of cardboard. Stick splodges of wet tissue over the cardboard and then cover with layers of papier-mâché (see page 56).

2 Paint with white emulsion paint. Smooth out metallic sweet papers until they are flat and then stick them on to the nodules on the crown.

3 Paint the crown gold and then stick diamanté decorations all over it. Add patterns in silver pen. Thread elastic at the back to hold it on the head.

A Knight's Helmet

A helmet is easy to make out of papier-mâché (see page 56), building it up over a balloon. Blow up a balloon and then cover it with five or six layers of papier-mâché. When the papier-

mâché is dry, pop the balloon and cut away the front of the helmet to accommodate the face. Add a yogurt pot upside down to the top of the helmet. Cover the whole thing with another coat of papier-mâché, paint it silver and finally add a feather to the top.

A Damsel's Hat

Cut a conical hat from card, as if making a witch's hat (see page 19), but before folding the hat into a cone shape, glue on a metallic fabric or spray with gold or silver. Cut a strip of net or a fine fabric and gather it round the bottom in swags and stick sequins on the front of the hat. Make a hole about the size of a ping pong ball at the top, cut a long piece of netting and poke it into the top, letting the rest flow down to the floor.

A Knight's Shield

A shield can be made from a large, empty washing powder box. Draw an oval, round or heart-shaped outline on the back of the box and cut it out. Cut the top off the box with the handle and stick this on to the back of the shield. To decorate the shield, either spray it with silver or cover in foil and then draw on a design and paint it with poster paints. You may wish to make up your own coat of arms or paint on the wearer's initials.

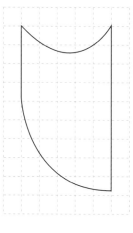

FUN IN THE JUNGLE

Here's an opportunity to dress up as wild beasts of the jungle! Or you can make jungle costumes from animal print fabrics worn over swimming costumes with flower garlands. To add to the jungle atmosphere, why not make some green crêpe paper creepers and large tissue paper butterflies and flowers? Trees can be made from cardboard tubes painted green with large green cartridge paper leaves stuck on.

Making the Costumes

★ **Make tiger and leopard print costumes using the all-in-one pattern on pages 58–60 and the hood pattern featured on page 61.**

Other Ideas

★ A monkey tail is easily made from fake fur and fabric and then stitched on to a leotard.

★ For a parrot costume, wear brightly coloured tights and a T-shirt. You can add a green hood with an orange beak to give a truly authentic look – just follow the instructions on page 61.

★ To complete the parrot, make paper wings and paint in bright colours.

If you are having a jungle fancy-dress party, decorate the room with paper trees and butterflies.

Butterfly

★ **For a butterfly costume, wear a black leotard and tights.**
★ **Make wings from a sheet of fabric decorated with fabric paints or appliqué. Attach on to the leotard at the shoulders, and tack down the middle of the back.**

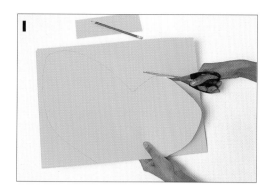

Making a Pair of Wings

1 Fold an A1 sheet of coloured card in half and using the template on page 63 as a guide, draw on the butterfly wings, making sure the straight edge of each wing lies on the fold in the card. Cut out the wings, and don't forget to cut out the tab as well. Open out the wings.

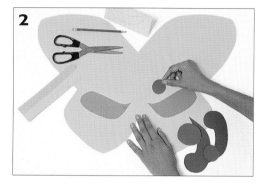

2 Cut out various shapes from brightly coloured gummed paper. Dampen and stick on to the front and back of the wings.

3 Using sticky tape, secure the card tab along the crease in the centre of the wings, leaving the top and the bottom ends open. Use these openings to thread through two lengths of black elastic through the tube created by the tab. Tie the ends of the elastic together to form loops for the child's arms to go through.

A GAME TO PLAY

Animal search

This is an alternative to the popular game of hunt the thimble and goes down a treat with younger children who have dressed up as animals and are pretending to be in a jungle.
You will need Six or more animal shapes cut out of plain coloured paper – enough different species for each child who is going to be playing the game. The shapes should be obvious to identify (like elephants, monkeys and lions) so if you run out of easy shapes, cut out birds, butterflies,

snakes, tortoises or whatever as well). Hide all the paper shapes around the house. If there are any rooms that are out of bounds, close the door and put up a notice saying 'keep out' or tell the children which rooms they are allowed to search.
To play You can either tell the children to find one of each animal, or tell them to find all the shapes of one particular animal. The winner is the first person to find all the shapes they have been asked to look for.

Nursery Rhymes

Here is a great opportunity to be your favourite nursery rhyme character. You can be Goldilocks or one of the three bears, Little Red Riding Hood or the Big Bad Wolf. Simple masks and props will allow you to be anything you want to be!

MAKING THE COSTUMES

★ Make a teddy hood out of fake fur using the pattern on page 61.

★ Use the all-in-one pattern on pages 58–60 to make the body of the teddy.

★ For a simpler costume, attach round ears made from fake fur lined in pink felt to a headband and blacken your nose.

★ Wear brown woollen mittens for paws.

★ Make a teddy mask from card covered in felt.

Making Little Red Riding Hood's Cloak

1 For the cloak, follow the instructions on page 57. For the hood, cut a smaller circle of red fabric and cut in half. Sew the two halves together along the straight edge of the semicircle.

2 Insert a piece of ridgeline or boning along that seam – this will make the hood stand out around the face.

3 Gather the two sections of material from the semicircle and sew them on to the neckline of the cloak. Sew over the raw edges on the front and hem of the cloak to neaten up. Add red ribbon ties at the neck.

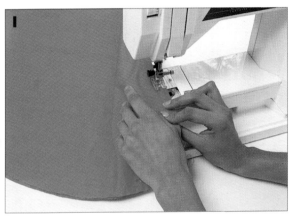

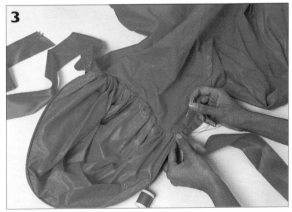

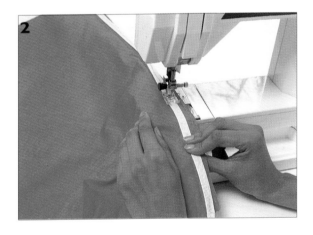

Other Ideas

★ A fierce wolf mask can be made from card covered in grey felt.

★ Little Red Riding Hood's dress can simply be a pretty party dress with frills.

★ To dress up as Little Miss Muffet, wear a mobcap made from a 75cm (30in) circle of fabric with elastic inserted 10cm (4in) from the outside edge to make a frill. To complete the outfit, carry a bowl and spoon for curds and whey and a plastic spider.

★ Simple Simon's pie man only needs to wear a chef's apron and carry a tray of pies.

★ Make the little pig mask as described opposite.

Making a Pig Mask

1 Hold a paper plate up to your face and mark the position of your eyes, nose and mouth with a pencil. Cut out the eye holes. Attach a length of black elastic.

2 To make a nose, squash a small fromage frais carton and stick it on the plate. Paint the plate and the nose pink and add a pink mouth with a felt pen.

3 Cut out pink felt ears and attach to the back of the mask.

4 The finished mask.

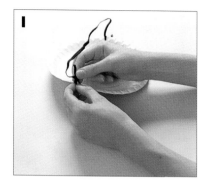

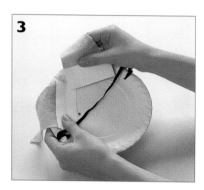

GAMES TO PLAY

Pretending to be nursery rhyme characters and playing games on this theme naturally appeal to younger children.

Nursery rhyme charades

To play Everyone sits in a circle and you ask if there is anyone who would like to act out a nursery rhyme for the others to guess. You have to explain that no talking is allowed and everyone has got to pretend. Some children will find it easy to think of a suitable rhyme but younger children may need you to whisper a suggestion to them such as 'Humpty Dumpty'. In this case, you whisper to the child that he or she should go into the middle of the circle and pretend to sit on an imaginary wall and then fall off. Tell them to do their mime again until one of the others guesses correctly and it becomes their turn.
Here are some other suggestions:
Little Miss Muffet would sit on an imaginary chair pretending to eat from a bowl and then looking frightened and running away from an imaginary spider. Jack Horner is easy to act out: sitting in a corner, putting a thumb in a pretend pie, and then pulling out his thumb and looking smug and smiling. Prizes should be awarded for each successful act.

Ring-a-ring o' roses

Even shy children who are very young will be happy to join in this game to break the tension at the beginning of a party.
To play All the children hold hands and walk or skip around in a circle while singing the nursery rhyme 'Ring-a-ring o' roses'. If you want to make it into more of a game, when it comes to the traditional 'All fall down' part of the song, then the last child to fall down is out. This continues until there is only one child left who is declared the winner and given a prize.

Create your very own Jurassic Park or Land That Time Forgot by dressing up as a caveman or dinosaur. To make the costumes, use scraps of fake fur or brown fabric and, for dinosaur masks, use cardboard and egg boxes. You could also design your very own caveman drawings on the walls of your cave!

MAKING THE COSTUMES

★ Sew together bits of fake fur, suede, or leather scraps using zigzag stitching to make male or female cave costumes.

★ Make a club by following the instructions (right).

★ Make a dinosaur body from a long length of green fabric, gathered at the neck with elastic. Cut armholes so the dinosaur can use his hands!

★ Make a pterodactyl hood by using the pattern on page 61 and attach felt spikes along the top.

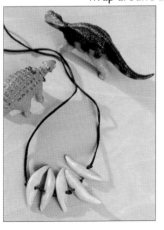

Making a Caveman's Costume

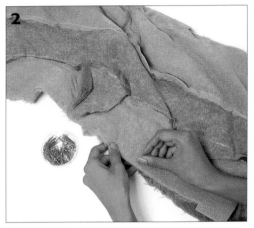

1 Gather together scraps of fake fur, suede and leather. Cut the scraps into long strips, then using a sewing machine, zigzag stitch these pieces together until you have a rectangular 'skin' which is large enough to wrap around a child's body.

2 Fold this piece in half and then sew the ends together, so you are left with a large tube which the child can slip over his or her head.

3 Add two straps, or cut armholes in the tube.

★ If you can find a bought necklace of what look like real dinosaur teeth (left) it will add the finishing touch to a cave costume. Otherwise it is quite easy to make a tooth necklace by shaping teeth in papier-mâché (see page 56) and stringing them together on a piece of string or a leather shoelace.

You can make a club simply by rolling a broadsheet newspaper into a tube, halving it and sticking the two pieces together with masking tape to make a handle. Blow up a small balloon and cover it with three layers of papier-mâché (see page 56). When the papier-mâché is dry, pop the balloon, cut a hole in the side of the club head and insert the handle. Fasten securely in place with masking tape and add another layer of papier-mâché over the top of the whole thing. Decorate the club with brown paint and then apply a coat of clear varnish.

Make Your Own Cave

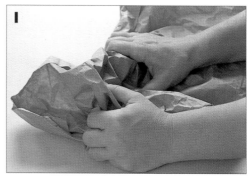

1 Crumple brown paper to give the natural uneven look of caves and stick inside a large box which has been placed on its side.

2 Sponge brown and terracotta paints over the cave 'walls'.

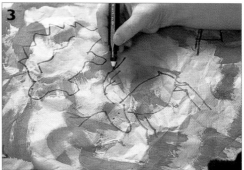

3 The cave is ready for decorating by the cavemen! Using fine black felt pens, draw stick men with spears on to the brown wrapping paper.

Basic Techniques & Patterns

Papier-Mâché

Papier-mâché is the ideal substance for making models, costumes and props. It can be worked on a balloon, on chicken wire, on to cardboard and plastic containers, or it can be moulded into simple shapes. Papier-mâché is very simple to decorate and a final coat of varnish ensures it will last.

Papier-mâché is basically paper and glue. For all the props in this book I have used newspaper and wallpaper paste. You can, however, use PVA diluted 50:50 with water. This gives a very strong finish, or you can use a flour and water paste.

To make flour and water paste, you need 1 mug of water and 3 mugs of flour. In a saucepan, mix a little of the water with the flour until you have a smooth paste and then add the rest of the water slowly, stirring all the time. Heat the mixture until it boils and let it simmer until the paste thickens. Turn the heat off and use when cold.

To papier-mâché

1 Rip newspaper into strips about 2.5cm (1in) wide. Dip the paper into glue and then squeeze off the excess between thumb and forefinger.

2 Apply the paper strips on to the base you are using. Work one layer at a time and allow to dry between layers. Five or six layers are usually enough for any project.

3 When dry, paint with a coat of white emulsion before decorating.

Costumes

From three basic patterns you can make most fancy dress costumes you are ever likely to need. A tabard can be used for a red Indian dress, a Peter Pan, elf or pixie, a soldier, or even a painting smock. A cloak can be for a wizard, a witch, a knight, a lady, Little Red Riding Hood and a conjuror. An all-in-one may be an animal, a racing driver, a clown or a space man.

To make a jacket or trousers, use the top or bottom of the all-in-one pattern and add a generous seam allowance at the waist or hem to allow for alterations.

For a skirt, make a tube of material with an elasticated top which can be adjusted to the size of the wearer.

Cloak

For a photographic step-by-step sequence see page 18.

1 To make a full cloak you will need a large square of fabric: 135cm x 135cm (54in x 54in). Fold the square in half and place against the child's shoulder; this will show how long the cloak will be. Open out the material.

2 Fold the square in half and half again.

3 Draw a small curve on the corner with the folds for the neck and a large curve on the opposite corner for the hem.

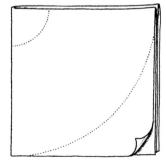

4 Cut along the curves.

5 Open out the material. You will have a large circle with a hole in the centre. Cut a straight line from the small circle to the large one. This is the front of the cloak.

6 Fold over 6mm ('/4in) of the raw edges and hem to neaten. Add ribbon ties at the neck.

7 If you wish to add a collar, measure the length of the neck and cut a piece of fabric this length plus 12mm ('/2in) seam allowance, by double the depth you wish the collar to be.

8 Sew the collar on to the neck along one long side of the collar, right sides together. Fold the collar down and sew the other long side on to the neck, hiding any raw edges. Neaten the edges of the collar by turning them in and sewing by hand.

9 To make a hood, cut a smaller circle (68cm [27in]) of fabric and cut in half. With right sides facing, sew the two halves together down their straight edge. Sew a piece of ridgeline or boning along the inside of the seam. This will make the hood stand out around the face. Stitch together and gather the double thickness of the semicircle and sew it on to the neck line.

Simple Cloak

Instead of using a circle, this method uses a rectangle of fabric. Make a channel along one of the narrow ends to carry elastic or drawstring.

Neaten the bottom and sides with a hem or running stitch. Fasten the cloak with a button or drawstring. For a knight, appliqué a shield on the back.

Tabard

1 To calculate the amount of fabric needed, measure from the shoulder to the knee, add 5cm (2in) for seam allowance and double the measurement.

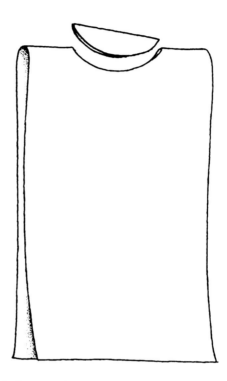

2 Cut your length of fabric, fold it in half and cut a hole large enough to fit over the child's head. If you wish, cut a further slit down the front of about 10cm (4in) and make holes either side of the slit for lacing.

3 Neaten round the neck and the sides of the tabard. You can sew up the sides if you wish, but leave lots of room for the arms to move easily. Cut a fringe for an Indian dress and a zigzag pattern for a pixie. Decorate according to the costume you are making.

4 If you are not sewing up the sides, sew on ribbon or bias binding tape ties at the sides.

BASIC PATTERNS

All-in-one

From this pattern you can make every conceivable kind of animal as well as making a clown and a spaceman.

The pattern fits a 4- to 6-year-old but can be enlarged by lengthening the body section. Each piece incorporates a 15mm ($^5/_8$in) seam allowance.

1 Enlarge the pattern given here on to dressmakers' grid paper or photocopy it. Check that the arms and legs fit your child.

2 Cut out two fronts, two backs, and two sleeves (see page 60) for each costume.

3 With right sides facing, sew the two fronts together as far as the dot.

Step 3

4 Sew in poppers, velcro or a zip down the rest of the front seam.

5 With right sides facing, sew the two backs together down the centre back seam. If making an animal, leave a gap for the tail.

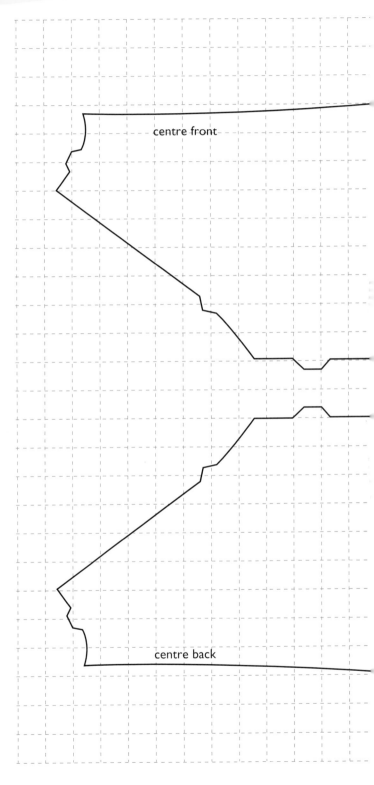

centre front

centre back

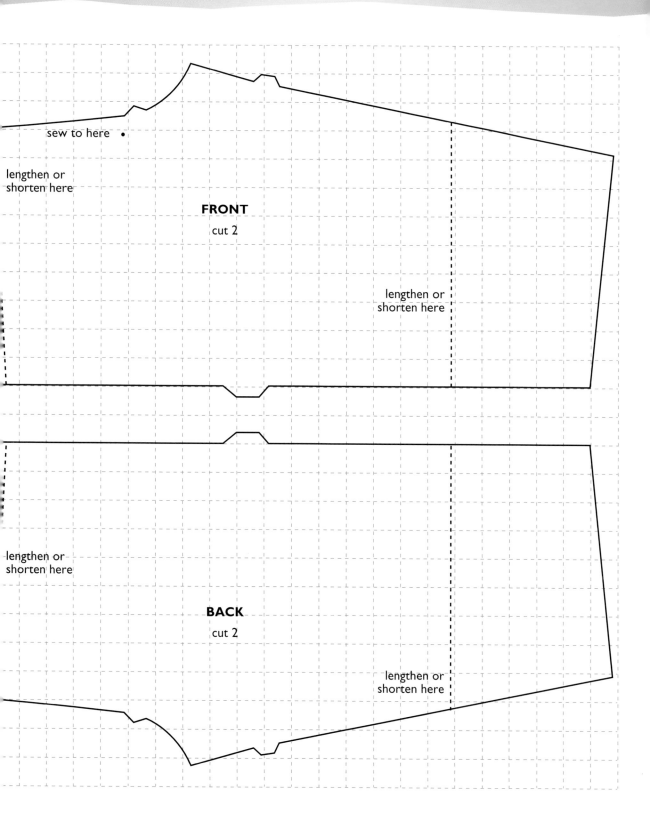

sew to here •

lengthen or
shorten here

FRONT

cut 2

lengthen or
shorten here

lengthen or
shorten here

BACK

cut 2

lengthen or
shorten here

BASIC PATTERNS

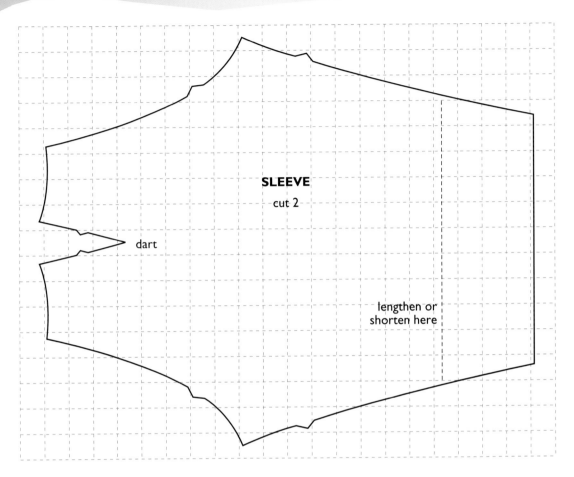

SLEEVE

cut 2

dart

lengthen or
shorten here

6 Sew the darts on the shoulder seams. Pin the sleeves to the edges of the armholes front and back. Sew into position.

7 Sew down all the seams. For a spaceman add metallic cuffs and complete the outfit with a silver foil backpack and crash helmet. For a clown cut the pattern in different coloured and patterned materials. Add patch pockets and a ruff collar.

Step 6

Step 7

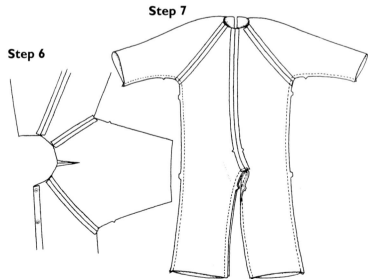

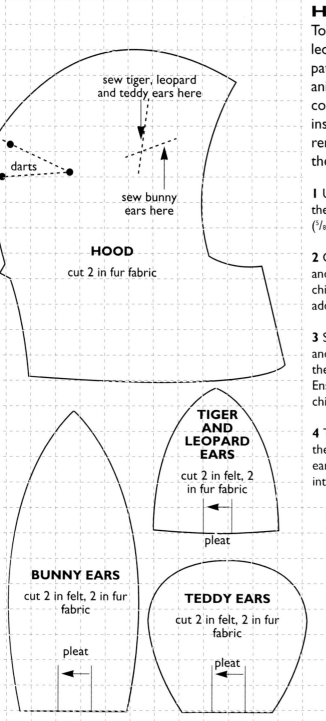

Hoods

To make the bunny, chick, teddy bear, tiger and leopard hoods featured in this book, use the pattern pieces (left and below). Whichever animal hood you decide to make, choose the correct colour fake fur and then follow the instructions below. When cutting fur fabric, remember to make sure the pile is all going in the right direction.

1 Using 2.5cm (1in) squared paper, draw and cut out the relevant pattern pieces. Each piece has a 15mm (⁵⁄₈in) seam allowance included in the outline.

2 Cut two hood shapes from fur, two ears from fur and a further two ears from lining fabric or felt. For a chick, cut two beaks from orange felt and an additional beak shape from interfacing.

3 Sew the darts on each piece, right sides together, and then sew the two head pieces together around the curved seam – again, with right sides together. Ensure that you leave space to fit the hood over the child's head.

4 To make the ears, with right sides together stitch the pleats and then sew the felt linings to the fur ears. Turn right sides out and then stitch the ears into place as indicated on the pattern.

5 For the chick, iron the interfacing on to one side of one of the beaks and then sew the beaks together with the interfacing sandwiched between them. Sew the beak into place as in the photograph on page 9.

61

BASIC PATTERNS

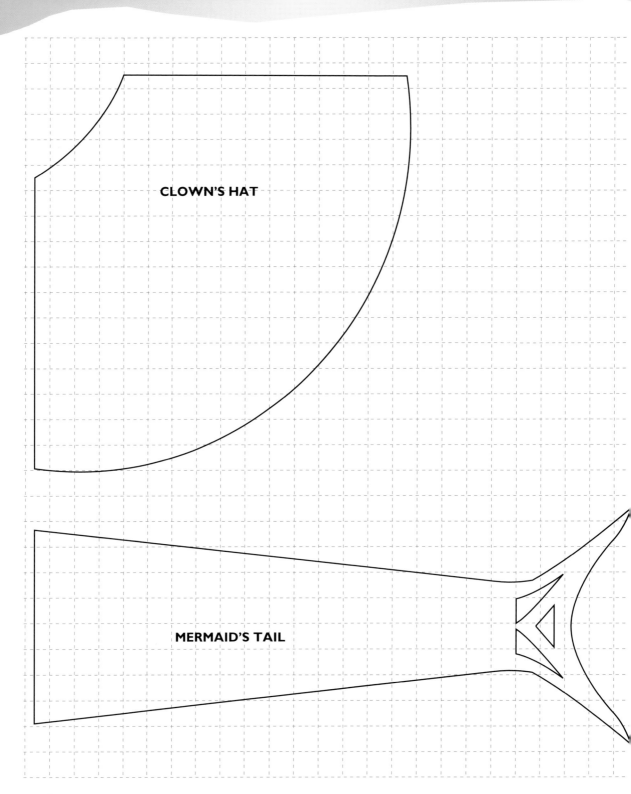

CLOWN'S HAT

MERMAID'S TAIL

FLOWER HEADBAND

BUTTERFLY WING

FLOWER COLLAR

INDEX